# HOW TO BECOME A WEALTHY CATALYST

## The Step- By- Step Guide To Transforming Your Consulting Career Into Wealth

Gerhart Banks

# Table Of Contents

*Marketing strategies*

# INTRODUCTION

# The purpose of this manual

Among the wide range of professional pursuits, where every career path is distinct, **consulting** is a field with virtually endless opportunities. ***Imagine this:*** You, the main character in your narrative, negotiating the complex world of consulting. You have a set of abilities that allow you to solve problems, *but what if these abilities also held the key to an incredible wealth trove?*

***We start our story with you,*** a gifted person with a strong desire to succeed and be prosperous. You have navigated the waters of consulting, and although opportunity abounds, the road to financial success may appear hazy. This is where our guide comes into play, a compass to help you make your way through the complex map of turning your consulting career into a fulfilling journey.

*You may wonder why you need this guide.* To put it another way, picture it as the sage advisor in every great story—the Dumbledore to Harry Potter, the Gandalf to Frodo. Your journey through the consulting industry is not like any other adventure; rather, it is a story that has yet to be told, one that will be full of obstacles, victories, and riches that surpass the ordinary.

First of all, think of this manual as your career's treasure map, guiding you through unknown territory. The business environment is dynamic, and taking the traditional path may not always result in striking gold. But this guide is your magical parchment, illuminating the hidden passageways and doors that lead to affluent realms.

Let's now explore the central theme of our story. Consider your consulting career as a journey, every project as a task to be accomplished, and every client as a persona in your narrative. ***You come to understand that conventional maps and SOPs*** are inadequate as you progress through these quests. A guide who is knowledgeable about the subtleties of this exceptional journey is required, one who can turn your consulting misadventures into a prosperous story.

The protagonist of our story is presented with a crucial decision in the opening chapter: to follow the traditional path or to accept the call for change. This mentor takes on the role of the sage old man, bestowing upon the main character a magical amulet that will open doors to a world in which consulting is more than just business dealings—it's about creating an empire of enduring wealth.

Just like the protagonist did once, you might wonder, ***"Why do I need this guide?"*** That is, since this is more than just a how-to manual.

With every project, choice, and encounter with a client, you write your legend. It involves more than just finding solutions to issues; it involves creating a successful fabric that transcends the ordinary.

Let's now explore the chapters that contribute to this guide's captivating story. In the grand scheme of consulting, it's not just about making money; it's also about figuring out your specialty, or USP. The protagonist is given a mirror by the guide, which reflects their latent potential, passions, and strengths. It promotes the understanding that to be unique within the large network of consultants, one must weave a tale that is impossible for others to duplicate.

As the story develops, our guide takes on the role of a mentor and emphasizes the value of knowledge. True wisdom becomes rare in an era of abundant information. The main character discovers that mastering their chosen field is not only a desirable objective but also a requirement. It's the spell that enchants clients, the enchanted sword that slays rivals, and the potion that turns routine projects into extraordinary triumphs.

And without a compelling character, what good is a captivating story? Our guide leads the main character on a quest to develop a personal brand that appeals to peers and clients alike. The main character discovers that in the wide ocean of professional relationships, a strong personal brand is more than just a symbol—it's a beacon that draws opportunities, alliances, and admirers.

The networking chapter builds upon itself as the guide goes along. Imagine the protagonist mixing with other figures from the business world at a lavish ball held in a castle straight out of a fairy tale. The protagonist's journey is elevated by networking, which turns into a symphony of conversations and connections akin to a magical ballroom dance. The guide teaches the art of effective networking, or converting random meetings into strategic alliances, while also providing the dance moves.

As the protagonist learns the secret to producing extraordinary outcomes, the story takes an exciting turn. According to the guide, every project is an opportunity to demonstrate brilliance rather than just a task to be completed. The main character discovers that happy customers are more than simply your sponsors—they are the storytellers who carry your legend to the remote corners of the consulting realm.

The guide then provides access to further benefits. Think of this as the turning point where the main character learns a new talent or weapon that enhances their consulting expertise. Workshops, courses, or educational materials turn into enchanted objects that not only benefit customers but also generate new revenue streams, boosting the protagonist's finances.

The narrative voice, who serves as our guide, then muses on the subject of scalability—the idea of creating procedures and systems that let the protagonist's company expand like a legendary beast. Technology, outsourcing, and automation work like magic to turn a one-person show into a thriving empire.

The protagonist enters the stage of marketing and sales as the narrative comes to a head. The guide takes on the role of a playwright, creating scenes and dialogue that connect with the clients, who make up the audience. The main character discovers that sales are about establishing long-lasting relationships, and marketing is about telling an engaging story rather than just making sales.

As the story comes to an end, the guide transforms into a financial advisor who teaches the protagonist how to manage the kingdom's finances. Financial objectives, investments, and budgets serve as the keys to opening the wealth-storage vaults. The main character comes to understand that creating a prosperous legacy is just as important to a successful consulting career as generating revenue.

The guide takes on the role of the librarian in the penultimate chapter, promoting lifelong learning. The main character is aware that remaining current is not only a matter of choice but also a necessity in a world where information truly is power. The guide opens the door to a world of limitless opportunities where learning new things is an exciting journey that never ends.

As the mentor advises the protagonist to diversify sources of income, the climax draws near. Investing, forming alliances, and expanding into related fields serve as the enchanted linkages that span various spheres of prosperity. The main character comes to understand that building a symphony of revenue streams is the key to true wealth, rather than relying solely on one source.

The guide then assumes the role of the knowledgeable elder in the last chapter, advising the protagonist to give back and expand their network. The protagonist is aware that achieving success requires teamwork rather than just going it alone. Contributing to the community and establishing connections with powerful people turn into heroic actions that make the main character a legendary figure.

The protagonist is left standing at the summit of success, surrounded by the riches of wealth, knowledge, and meaningful relationships, as the guide bids farewell in the epilogue. Despite its share of difficulties, the trip has been a life-changing adventure; it's the tale of a consulting career transformed into a prosperous odyssey.

When the main character shuts the guide, they understand that it is more than just a guide; rather, it is a dynamic story that they were writing with every task, choice they made, and encounter. As a treasured relic, the guide now serves as a symbol of the protagonist's journey and a continual reminder that wealth in the world

# Chapter One

## Identify your niche

A market niche is an area where specific goods and services are in high demand. Certain regions, cultures, events, or activities can be catered to by niche markets.

The specialized nature of services is growing these days. A deep understanding of one or two subjects is frequently preferable to a broad understanding of everything. Specialization provides information about your company's operations to clients, investors, and business partners. ***The following method will assist you step-by-step:***

- **1. Determine your areas of passion.**

A critical first step is identifying your interests. During your leisure time, what do you do? What topics do you enjoy learning about? Perhaps it's time to change careers if your work is in an area you find boring. Remaining motivated is easier when you enjoy your work more, but growing into and keeping a new role is difficult.

- **2. Determine the issues that you can resolve**

Resolving the issues of a client base is the primary objective of any business or service. Don't forget to conduct market research and brainstorm. An excellent resource for brainstorming ideas is Google Trends, which is free of cost. Look for gaps in the market after determining what interests you.

- **3. Give each person priority**

It is acceptable if not everyone purchases what you are offering. Rather than attempting to reach everyone, what matters is identifying the appropriate clients. Seeking individuals who align with your principles will increase brand loyalty and increase the likelihood of a successful business.

- **4. Conduct a Test**

Typically, you don't buy the first pair of shoes you try on when shopping for shoes. Search around and find something that works. Finding your niche is no different.

It is possible that you would like to manage an online store or business. In that scenario, try to find strategies to direct customers to your small business through search engine optimization.

- **5. Gather feedback**

Speak with people if you're unsure. To get opinions and insights, you can consult your family or coworkers. Discuss the unique requirements of your target market with them. Seek out individuals in related fields or roles to begin networking.

- **6. Give up on generating revenue right away**

That is indeed the main objective of a marketing plan. It's best to avoid overstretching yourself financially when starting a new business, though.Making a profit can not happen quickly.

- **7. Examine Competitors**

Make sure that the work you produce is unique by making notes about other resources that can assist you with branding, content, and strategy.

- **8. Identify what makes your selling point unique.**

All services and businesses have a differentiator that sets them apart from the competition. Everything from the app's layout to a cookie's contents could be considered this. Your inventiveness can come through in this situation. Consider what distinguishes your offering.

- **9. Verify your concepts**

You should test your niche to determine whether it is appropriate. To exhibit your ideas and get exposure to other people, create a website, go door to door, or go to different business fairs.

- **10. Evaluate the niche you have chosen.**

Enhancement is perpetually possible. Revisit the following questions and respond:

•How profitable is your business idea?

•Your target audience is who?

•For customers, what solutions are you providing?

Well-run companies constantly evaluate and make necessary adjustments.

# How Should you position yourself as an Authority

Select an interest-driven topic for yourself. Do you regard someone as an authority on any subject, be it yoga, investing, do-it-yourself projects, or anything else?

Likely, the number of people you follow to obtain information will be relatively small. When it comes to information regarding the field you're interested in, you can rely on these experts.

Your trust in them stems from what? Why did they seem like experts to you?

- **Authority**

Being an expert requires a lot of work; this much cannot be avoided. A subject matter expert will have extensive knowledge of the subject and be able to articulate and illustrate concepts or information with ease.

- **The ability to adapt**

You will constantly come back to a true expert to get their opinion on new challenges or opportunities because they will be knowledgeable about current trends and discussions in their industry.

- **Audience**

How did you come upon that expert's work originally? Maybe a friend recommended them, or perhaps their most popular YouTube videos have garnered thousands of views. In any case, it's likely that you first became aware of them because other people were using them as authorities.

Gaining credibility in your industry and attracting people to your brand to get the information they need on subjects that are important to them can be achieved by mastering the balance of authority, flexibility, and audience trust.

# How to position yourself as an Authority

It takes a deliberate approach and persistent work to establish yourself as an authority in your field. Developing your expertise in a particular field should be your first step on this journey. It is simpler for others to identify your expertise when you have a distinct identity, which comes from specialization.

Make quality content regularly and share it. Spread knowledge that demonstrates your in-depth knowledge of your industry via social media, podcasts, and blogs. Identify pressing issues, offer creative solutions, and share success stories to establish yourself as a thought leader.

Participating in webinars or conferences as a public speaker increases the visibility of your work in the industry. Establish credibility by sharing your viewpoints, experiences, and knowledge. To further establish yourself as an acknowledged authority, consider writing a book or contributing to whitepapers.

Make sure your LinkedIn profile and business website are optimized to create a strong online presence. Join organizations that are pertinent to your industry, go to networking functions, and look for opportunities to work with influential people. To demonstrate the real-world effects of your experience, ask pleased customers or associates for testimonials.

Seize the chance to educate others by being proactive in looking for training sessions or workshops. Sharing your expertise strengthens your grasp of the topic while also helping others.

Continuity is essential. Keep up with industry developments, participate in discussions regularly, and share your insights. Make connections with experts in your field by being personable and accommodating.

Finally, think about doing pro bono work for nonprofit organizations. By giving up your knowledge, you can show off your abilities and build a larger network while also showcasing your dedication to making a positive impact on society.

By integrating these techniques, you'll establish yourself as a subject matter expert and further your field's progress while leaving a lasting legacy of influence and knowledge.

# Strategies for utilizing your reputation and brand

Making the most of the trust and recognition you have established in your business is a deliberate activity known as "leveraging your brand and reputation." Increasing your impact, growing your network, and creating new opportunities all depend on this process.

First and foremost, develop a powerful and unified personal brand. Make sure you have a clear understanding of your identity, values, and contributions. Establishing a recognizable and consistent image entails coordinating your visual identity, communication style, and internet presence. Invest in polished portfolios, LinkedIn profiles that are optimized, and well-designed logos as components of your professional branding.

Manage your reputation actively after that. To guarantee a favorable impression, keep an eye on mentions, reviews, and comments made online. Deal with any problems in a timely and competent manner. Reputation building demands a dedication to quality, dependability, and moral behavior. Reputation can be greatly enhanced by producing high-quality work regularly and keeping lines of communication open.

Use a variety of media to effectively promote your brand by demonstrating your skills. Compose articles, make contributions to trade journals, and use social media to communicate your thoughts. Become recognized as a thought leader by regularly producing insightful material that is in line with your brand's messaging. This helps you establish yourself as an authority in your field and strengthens your reputation.

A great strategy for increasing brand leverage is networking. Participate in online forums, go to industry events, and establish deep relationships with experts in your field. Work together with thought leaders and influencers, and look for chances to give talks or make guest appearances to share your knowledge. Your network has the power to enhance your reputation and brand, creating opportunities for joint ventures, collaborations, and professional growth.

Endorsements and testimonials are important resources for building brand power. Urge pleased customers, associates, or partners to share their great experiences. To increase credibility and foster confidence with prospective customers or employers, display these endorsements on your website or in other marketing materials.

Leveraging your brand and reputation requires consistency. Continue to interact with your audience, share new achievements, and review and update your online profiles regularly. This continuous work guarantees that your brand stays current and appeals to your intended market.

In summary, building a strong personal brand, a solid reputation, smart networking, thought leadership and the careful utilization of testimonials are all necessary components of a comprehensive approach to effectively leverage your brand and reputation. You set yourself up for more success, more visibility, and a wider effect on your professional activities when you actively manage and promote your brand.

# 7 pointers for scaling a company

While each company's business plan is different, those that scale well frequently adhere to many of the same best practices. With the help of these pointers, you may create a successful scaling strategy.

***The following seven pointers will help you as you grow your company:***

- **1. Plan your approach to boosting sales.**

Any company hoping to grow must prioritize increasing sales. Increasing the average revenue from existing clients or bringing on new ones are two ways to scale sales. Even while both strategies produce benefits, strengthening your bonds with present clients is frequently less expensive than bringing in new ones.

If your company is going to scale instead of grow, consider methods to boost sales while optimizing profit and avoiding the need for more resources.

***Among the top techniques to boost sales are:***

•Focus on a certain market

•Comprehend consumer behavior

•Respond to input from customers;

•Assemble a group of knowledgeable salespeople;

•Create a successful marketing strategy; use

•CRM software to handle leads and customer interactions; and

•Hone your messaging.

- **2. Make a tech investment**

According to a global survey by Automation Anywhere, manual administrative chores account for more than 40% of a worker's daily workload on average. Many of these duties can be automated with the correct technology, giving team members more time to concentrate on strategic priorities and larger business objectives.

*To grow your company, think about investing in technology to assist in the automation of duties and procedures like:*
•Employee onboarding
•Bookkeeping and salary
•Relationship management with customers
•Project oversight
•Arrangement of appointments
When considering automation as a means of growing your business, evaluate potential technology partners and suppliers according to important factors such as cost, time to market, customer support, and ease of use.

- **3. Grow your staff to meet the demands of the market**

Finding the abilities necessary to achieve your goals and identifying any skill gaps in your team are the first steps in building the team you need to grow your firm.

Consider the particular hard and soft abilities that will enable your company to achieve its goals and provide the best possible customer service. Hard skills are technical, quantifiable, job-specific abilities acquired via training and experience. Soft skills are personal qualities that enable people to lead by example, function well in a team, and fit in with the culture of a business.

***Hard and soft skills examples are as follows:***

•**Hard abilities:** Search engine optimization, coding, business analytics, visual design, and project management

•**Soft abilities:** Quickness, friendliness, correspondence, planning, and time management

Additionally, keep in mind that team leaders are in charge of giving instructions and making sure everyone in the team knows what has to be done to meet your business objectives.

***Some instances of leadership abilities are:***
•Listening intently
•Solving issues
•Relationship development
•The intelligence of emotion
•Assigning

### • 4. Seek outside aid

Many early-stage growing businesses have a small core staff that performs multiple responsibilities. However, expecting every team member to be a superb generalist could ultimately lead to costly errors and burnout. As your business expands, consider bringing in specialists to increase output and provide outcomes.

### • 5. Make a strategy with attainable objectives.

Companies that scale well find the ideal balance between establishing realistic yet difficult objectives. Unrealistic or unclear goals may cause team members to lose motivation, which might hinder their capacity to grow. Once the leadership group has agreed upon objectives, share your strategy with the whole group to elicit support and enthusiasm for participation.

- **6. Gain experience in management**

At your company, managers are in charge of inspiring team members, helping them reach individual goals, and holding them accountable for results. Success in scaling your organization can be directly impacted by the efficacy of individual managers. For this reason, managers from all departments must possess the necessary abilities to promote successful company outcomes.

Determine the most critical abilities that will help you grow your company, whether you're employing full-time employees, promoting managers, or training your present team members in management.

***Among the management abilities are:***
•Analytical reasoning
•Methodical organizing
•Time handling
•Change control
•Direction

## • 7. Concentrate the business's offerings

Businesses that prioritize growth above size concentrate on generating as much income as they can by targeting a broad audience with their services and consumers. Although this strategy can increase income initially, there are frequent hazards to long-term growth and scalability.

Focusing too much on acquiring new clients at the expense of existing ones can result in attracting clients who aren't the greatest fit for a company's offerings or failing to engage existing clients. It also makes it difficult for a company to become recognized as an authority in a particular market or set of problems.

***Here are some strategies for narrowing the scope of what your business offers:***

•Recognize your advantages and disadvantages.

•Establish a niche for your goods and services (considering the quantity and type of your clientele).

•Determine the overall market that you can reach.

•Evaluate the opposition

•Determine the difficulties your target market faces.

•Take note of the preferences and behavior of your current clients.

•Provide solutions and communications that target the issues that customers are facing.

MARKETING
SCALE
BUSINESS
PLAN
SCHEDULE
MARKETING

# Chapter Two

# Scalable System Implementation

The ability of your processes to function consistently at any growth rate and size, while also supporting exponential expansion, is implied by scalability. ***This is how it should be done correctly.***

in place aids in workflow management and boosts general efficiency. Assets might be transitory things like on-hand goods or raw materials, or they can be permanent things like equipment.

## #1: Develop An Effective System

Talent is rarely the only factor in a business's growth. It is possible, but it will be difficult at every turn if there isn't a productive structure in place.

That just isn't a growth-promoting environment.

A plan and the appropriate resources to carry it out are the foundation of any good company operation. Scalable businesses use standard best practices and systems that are documented, and proven, and increase productivity while lowering costs without compromising performance or quality.

## #2: Acquire And Use Capital

If you don't have an endless supply of money, you will need to draw investors to your business. Real estate investors take advantage of chances by funding their acquisitions and optimizing return on investment using the money of others.

Businesses that exhibit growth potential and high returns are the only ones that attract investors. Speaking is one thing, and it can arouse interest.

## #3: Make Use Of Automations

One of the secrets to scalability is automation. Implementing a robust asset management system facilitates workflow management and boosts overall productivity. Assets might be transitory things like on-hand goods or raw materials, or they can be permanent things like equipment.

Knowing your assets and how they contribute to your financial viability is crucial for any size organization. This will enhance scalability in addition to the following benefits:

- Keep employees content and focused by providing them with the tools and equipment they require and making sure it's in good working order.
- Prevent theft and the expense of replacing assets.
- Avoid excessive maintenance expenditures by keeping track of each asset's location and state.
- Lower risk and liability;
- Maintain your spending plan;
- Provide superior goods and services

## #4: Create  Strong Basis

Efficiency and scalability in modern companies are based on technology. Apps and software that offer the right framework for expansion can be purchased for less money along the road.

Seek for methods and automation that can grow without raising acquisition or manufacturing expenses.

**Examples include selecting** a pay-as-you-grow platform or a SaaS service over a standalone platform that requires ongoing updates and maintenance. You can then control growth and prevent significant interruptions.

## #5: Select And Grow Excellent Talent

There is more to strategic asset management than only making use of tangibles like tools and equipment. Human resources are among your most important assets.

What kind of talent will your company require to fill the new positions brought about by the expansion? Do you have the technology and a workable business plan to back it up?

With the correct technology, you can concentrate on bringing in and nurturing leaders instead of getting bogged down in the day-to-day details of managing your business.

# Optimal approach to financial management

The portion of your business plan devoted to employing financial facts and projections to contextualize the remainder of your plan is known as financial management, or planning. Predicting your company's future financial performance is the rationale behind financial management. Three essential procedures are essential to this function:

- Financial Forecasting
- Stress testing essential inputs needed to propel your expansion

- Getting ready for the funding requirements your company will require.

## What are the strategies for financial management?

In essence, financial management strategies are broad guidelines that your business can use to optimize the performance of its financial systems and procedures. These tactics are adaptable to the unique objectives, requirements, and financial resources of your business.

Maximizing an organization's financial worth is the primary objective of financial management methods. These tactics handle all other financial activities and decisions that may have an impact on strategic financial decisions, as well as assess past financial performance, project future financial performance, and plan capital structure.

In summary, finance strategy essentially aids in creating a road map that businesses may use to control the utilization, accessibility, and distribution of resources. To guarantee comprehensive advancement, it strives to harmonize financial management with the corporate and business objectives of a firm.

## Why are financial Strategies plans crucial?

The benefit of using financial management techniques is that they can assist you in creating a successful business plan. It assists you in creating a set of guiding principles that will allow your business to run as efficiently as possible.

A business strategy is essentially predicated on financial strategy at its core. The assets, cash flow, and liabilities of an organization are inevitably taken into consideration in practically all business decisions. Every business plan needs to handle the following:

present revenue, annual tax payments, fund procurement schedules, external financing requirements, and current cash flow. Creating a business plan requires knowing exactly what financial goals you want to pursue and how they align with your overall vision. In essence, developing a business plan without a financial plan might be challenging.

Financial techniques assist you in determining whether your objectives are doable, overcoming unforeseen obstacles, and tracking your spending. In addition to this, financial plans support other facets of corporate strategies such as:

**The state of finances right now.**
- Determining any threats to the present financial state of your business.
- Determining whether funding is required for operations or expansions.

- Determining and establishing short-term financial objectives.

# Financial strategy types

- **1. The dividend approach**

The dividend strategy is a financial technique used to calculate the percentage of profits that should be delivered to shareholders after keeping some profits as excess for potential future investments.

- **2. Planning for capital structures**

A company's capital structure is made up of its debt capital, preference capital, equity capital, and retained earnings. A company's capital structure plans are designed to balance the benefits and drawbacks, or risks, of debt, preferred, and equity capital.

- **3. Planning for working capital**

Capital planning techniques are the last but certainly not the least. Working capital planning strategies are financial management techniques that assist in managing the need,

procurement, allocation, and future of cash in
your business.

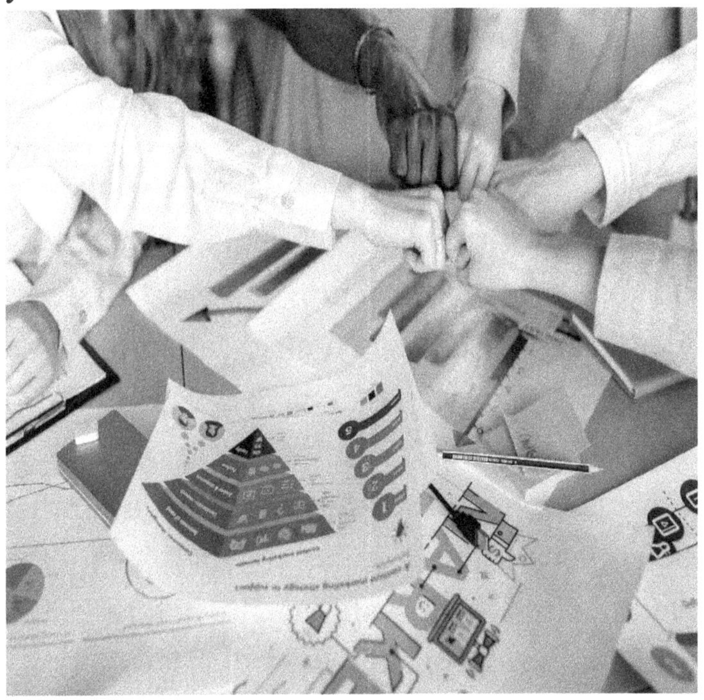

# Chapter Three

## What is the Cash Conversion Cycle (CCC)

The time (measured in days) it takes a business to turn its investments in inventory and other resources into cash flows from sales is expressed by a metric called the cash conversion cycle (CCC). The CCC, also known as the net operating cycle or just the cash cycle, quantifies the length of time that each net input dollar spends in the manufacturing and sales cycle before being turned into cash received.

This measurement considers the amount of time the business requires to sell its merchandise, collect outstanding payments from customers, and settle its debts.

The CCC is one of many quantitative metrics used to assess how well a business is managed and its operations run. A consistent downward trend in CCC values over time is encouraging, however, upward trends should prompt further research and analysis depending on other variables. Remember that CCC only applies to certain industries that rely on inventory management and related activities.

# The Cash Conversion Cycle Formula (CCC)

The currency conversion life cycle **(CCC)** mathematical formula can be expressed as follows since it includes determining the net aggregate time required for each of the three steps mentioned above.

**Where:** $CCC = DIO + DSO - DPO$

Days of Inventory Outstanding, or Days Sales of Inventory, is what DIO stands for.

Days Sales Outstanding, or DSO

Days Payable Outstanding (DPO)

**DPO** is connected to the company's cash outflow, whereas **DIO** and **DSO** are related to its cash inflows. **DPO** is the sole negative number in the computation as a result. An alternative interpretation of the formula construction could be that **DIO** and **DSO** are associated with inventory and accounts receivable, respectively, which are viewed as positive short-term assets. Accounts payable, a liability that is seen negatively, is connected to **DPO**.

# What the Cash Conversion Cycle Teaches You

The main strategy for a business to increase profits is to increase inventory sales. But how can one increase their sales? Regularly having access to cash makes it easier to turn a profit because there are more things to produce and sell when capital is readily available. Inventory purchases made by a business on credit may result in accounts payable **(AP)**.

Additionally, a business may sell goods on credit, generating accounts receivable **(AR).** As a result, unless the business settles the accounts payable and collects the accounts receivable, cash is irrelevant. Thus, a crucial component of financial management is timing.

The life cycle of money utilized for business activities is tracked by **CCC**. It tracks the cash as it is initially transformed into accounts payable and inventory, then into costs associated with developing new goods or services, on to sales and accounts receivable, and finally back into cash on hand. In essence, CCC shows how quickly a business can turn invested funds from the beginning (investment) to the finish (returns). ***It is preferable if the CCC is lower.***

## How to Differentiate Your Products Against Your Rivals

It's really difficult to stay relevant in a highly competitive industry.

especially in cases where the notion of **"brand diversity"** is inappropriate.

 For this reason, a lot of companies think that diversifying their product offerings is a good way to grow.

To put it simply, having a well-defined plan for expansion and growth enables you to investigate novel avenues for expanding the brand's reach into new markets, boosting sales and profits, and stabilizing financial results.

Adding a new feature, launching a new product, or adding a new sibling to an already-existing product line are all examples of product diversification. It might also refer to rebranding an already-existing product and entering a new market.

## Brands diversify; why?

Diversification serves various purposes, the primary one being to differentiate oneself from competitors. It is also beneficial to address many factors, including:

**Survival**— When sales of a certain product are declining, businesses might use diversification tactics to boost sales of the product.

**Adapting to change**—It only makes sense to diversify in light of recent advancements in research and technology as well as societal shifts that affect consumer behavior and demand.

**Want to go into a new or larger market—** One excellent strategy for a small firm to grow is by diversifying its product offering.

**Steer clear of overspecialization—** as this might impede an organization's expansion if it restricts sales to a particular market. Introducing new goods can be an excellent strategy to leave the field of specialization.

## These diversity types are as follows

**1. Concentric:** with this strategy, new goods or services are introduced that are comparable to those that already exist. To capitalize on the niche consumer base that prefers barista-style coffee at home, one strategy could be to move from selling coffee makers to businesses to selling coffee makers directly to consumers.

**2. Horizontal diversification:** this kind of diversification entails launching unrelated new items to the same clientele inside the same industry. For instance, a smartphone maker looking to enter a new market might start selling smartwatches.

**3. Conglomerate:** this refers to the process of developing new goods in many industries and outside the purview of the current offering. Johnson & Johnson, which sells consumer packaged products and medical devices, is a prime example.

# The most popular methods or strategies for diversification are:

**1. Extension:** By adding a new feature or feature to an existing product line, you can create a new version of the same product line. You could add a new flavor, like cashew, to your line of energy nut bits if, for example, you already sell four flavors—almond, hazelnut, pistachio, and coconut—and your base ingredient is almond. In a situation like this, the new flavor serves as an extra feature or element to draw in a new target market. Then, this cashew nut energy bite will join the family of products as a new sibling.

**2. Repackaging:** this is an additional strategy for product diversification. Just as with renaming, all you're doing here is giving your products better packaging. Given that 72% of consumers' purchasing decisions are influenced by packaging designs, a small modification could open up new sales opportunities. For example, you can alter the bottle or container design if you sell skincare or hair products.

**3. Renaming:** Renaming a product is a diversification tactic that might be useful if you want to enter a foreign market. In the current market, you can offer a product that is the same as the original, but you can rebrand it for the new market. For example, you can rename your flower bouquet business to reflect the culture of the new market you want to enter if you now offer it under a name that reflects the culture of your existing market.

**4. Resizing:** this is the process of making an existing product larger or smaller to better suit the demands of a new market. You can increase the number to sell in ten units if you sell a product in one, or vice versa. Sizing offers a plethora of imaginative choices. For example, you may provide the product in a travel size.

**5. Repricing:** Changing the cost of your goods is an additional way to diversify your offering. For instance, you could increase the price at which you sell premium or high-end products by making a manufacturing modification. Altering the ingredients slightly and selling them for less is another way to reduce the price.

**6. Brand extension:** Adding product diversity can be achieved by growing your brand of products by introducing a higher or lower end of the same product.

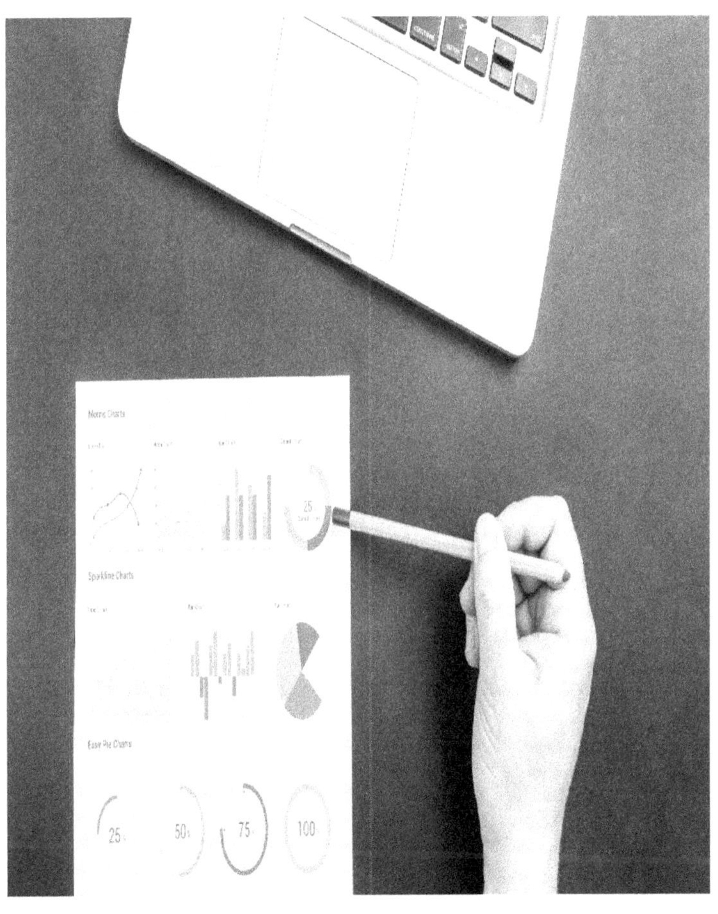

# Chapter Four

# What constitutes a business value

Value can refer to a quantity or a number, but it's most frequently used in finance to assess an asset's value as well as the financial performance of a business. A company's worth is estimated and anticipated by investors, stock analysts, and executives using a variety of financial criteria. Businesses can be evaluated according to their profit margin on a per-share basis, which is the profit divided by the total number of outstanding equity shares.

Valuation is the process of determining and allocating a value to an organization or an item. On the other hand, determining a stock price's fair worth is another application of the word valuation. Investment bank employees who analyze equity prices frequently perform valuations on companies to ascertain whether they are reasonably valued, undervalued, or overvalued about their present stock price and financial performance.

# Increasing the worth of your company

## 1. Seek counsel

Working with a knowledgeable outside advisor who can assist you in getting your company ready for sale, including getting an expert valuation done, is a good idea.

One of the most significant events in your life as an entrepreneur is selling your company. Expert guidance will assist in guaranteeing that you do it correctly.

## 2. Strive to increase your earnings

Large offers shouldn't be expected if you're barely breaking even.

Additionally, you don't want to withdraw too much cash from the company. Retained profits, or the part of net income that hasn't been paid to shareholders, show prospective investors that your company has been successful and is in good standing.

**3. Boost revenue and cut costs**

Examine your procedures and seek methods to improve operational effectiveness, reduce expenses, and manage inventories without compromising your business's operations. Revisit your marketing strategy and look for strategies to increase sales, such as entering new markets or introducing novel goods and services.

Concentrate on building a varied clientele that ideally brings in money regularly.

**4. Keep making improvements and investing**

Taking their foot off the accelerator after deciding to depart is one of the biggest blunders made by business entrepreneurs.

Your company's future value starts to decline the moment you cease making investments in maintenance, process enhancements, and new equipment.

## 5. Make a plan of action

A comprehensive plan including quantifiable objectives and benchmarks for the upcoming years helps establish your company's legitimacy as a developing enterprise with long-term potential.

## 6. Create standardized procedures and give your staff authority.

According to John Warrilow's book Built to Sell: Creating a Business That Can Thrive Without You, your company's procedures must be repeatable and teachable. "If your business can't function without you, you will have a hard time finding a buyer,"

Additionally, empower, inspire, and train your workforce. Focus especially on the management group. Strive to maintain a low staff turnover rate and work to resolve any internal problems. A competent and well-trained staff enhances the value of the company, particularly in those with little physical assets.

## 7. Make an impression on people

Selling your business is, in many respects, a marketing challenge unto itself. It's crucial to highlight to prospective customers what sets your good or service apart from the competitors. Request endorsements from a few of your devoted customers outlining their reasons for doing business with you and what attracts them to return.

# 10 Basic reasons valuation varies

Due to the intricate and ever-changing nature of the business environment, there are several reasons why business valuation could differ. The following are some important elements that influence how differently business values are valued:

- **Industry Structure:**

Valuation is influenced by the distinctive qualities of different sectors. Technology companies, for instance, might be valued differently from manufacturing companies because of things like market demand, growth potential, and intellectual property.

- **Market circumstances:**

Market demand, industry trends, and the state of the economy all have a big impact on firm valuation. In contrast to economic downturns, a business's valuation may vary during times of economic prosperity.

- **Performance Financially:**

The performance and financial stability of a company are what essentially determine its valuation. A greater valuation is influenced by factors like profitability, revenue growth, and stability; a lower valuation might be brought about by deteriorating performance.

- **Liabilities and Assets:**

The mix of a company's liabilities and assets might affect how much it is worth.

Businesses that have strong brand awareness, valuable intellectual property, or little debt may be valued more highly than those that have substantial liabilities.

- **Similars in the market:**

Comparing the target company's valuation to similar businesses in the market is a common practice. Comparable businesses may have differing growth prospects, risk profiles, or competitive advantages, which leads to variability.

- **Quality of Management:**

A company's valuation is influenced by the management team's skill and background. A more valuable asset may be a competent and established management group, which reflects the expectation of strong leadership.

- **Growth Expectations:**

Strong growth prospects typically translate into a greater valuation for a business than weak growth prospects. Businesses that are anticipated to grow and gain a greater market share are frequently paid more by buyers and investors.

- **The legal and regulatory landscape:** Law and regulation changes may affect firm valuation. Due to uncertainty and compliance costs, industries that undergo frequent regulatory changes may see more dramatic variations in their valuation.

- **Tangible Resources:** Enterprises possessing robust intangible assets, such as patents, copyrights, or a devoted clientele, could command premium prices. Businesses that possess distinct and justifiable competitive advantages are frequently valued higher by the market.

- **Market Attitude:** Business valuations can be impacted by market perceptions and investor mood. While negative sentiment can lead to undervaluation, positive sentiment may raise valuations.

To acquire an accurate and relevant valuation, it is essential to comprehend these aspects and do a thorough valuation analysis that takes into account the unique context of the organization.

## The only four methods of valuation you require

A business's worth can be fully understood through a variety of valuation techniques that take into account various aspects of its operations, finances, and market conditions. Here are four crucial techniques for valuation:

- **Cash Flow Discounted (DCF) Analysis:**

The DCF technique is a reliable approach to estimating a company's worth. It does this by projecting future cash flows and discounting them to their current value. This method provides a thorough evaluation of a company's intrinsic value while taking the time value of money into account. DCF is very helpful for companies with steady cash flow trends.

- **Analyzing Comparable Companies (CCA):**

In CCA, the target company's size, industry, and financial performance are compared to those of comparable publicly traded companies. To evaluate the target's valuation about its competitors, important indicators including the price-to-earnings (P/E) ratio, enterprise value-to-EBITDA (EV/EBITDA), and other multiples are used. This approach works well for companies that have distinct industry counterparts.

- **An analysis of precedent transactions**

Precedent transactions analysis is comparable to CCA in that it compares the target company to companies that have recently engaged in mergers or acquisitions. This approach provides a practical valuation benchmark by taking into account the purchase price paid for comparable businesses. It is particularly helpful for assessing companies in sectors where mergers and acquisitions occur often.

- **Asset-Based Assessment:**

The net asset value of a company is used in asset-based valuation to determine its value. It deducts liabilities and takes into account the company's tangible assets, which include things like real estate, inventory, and equipment. This approach is especially pertinent to companies in asset-heavy industries or those with important intellectual property. ***There are mostly two kinds:***

- The book value method values the balance sheet's assets at their historical cost.
- Values assets at their current market worth using the fair market value method.

The type of business, the state of the industry, and the goal of the valuation all influence the choice of valuation technique. These techniques are frequently combined to provide a more thorough and accurate business value.

# Chapter Five

# Optimal staging for sales

A business's selling preparations are a strategic dance that needs careful planning and execution. In addition to presenting the present, the choreography entails developing an engaging story for the future. Start with a comprehensive analysis of the company—know the finances, gauge the state of the market, and pinpoint opportunities for improvement. This prepares the groundwork for maximizing profitability and resolving any issues.

Next, clean up the company's outside. Optimize processes, polish financial reports, and take care of any outstanding legal or regulatory matters. Potential customers are not only drawn to but also given confidence by a well-kept business.

Write a futuristic story that will captivate readers. Clearly state the business's scalability, market differentiators, and growth prospects. Prospective buyers look for both current and future value.

Assemble a group of experts, such as financial counselors and attorneys, to handle the intricacies and guarantee a smooth procedure. Establish a data room filled with thorough paperwork so that prospective purchasers can get an intimate look at the background, performance, and prospects of the company.

And lastly, timing is everything. Sync the sale with the best possible market conditions, industry developments, and company success. Optimizing value and guaranteeing a smooth transition for all parties involved, a well-planned and executed sale turns the process from a transaction into a strategic move. Selling is only one aspect of it; another is planning a spectacular farewell that speaks to the company's history as well as its growth potential.

## Sales & Marketing That Works

Successful sales and marketing work together to create a smooth tango that draws in clients and turns them from potential into devoted consumers. A thorough understanding of the target audience is the foundation of this synergy. Marketing initiates the performance by developing engrossing storylines that align with the needs and goals of the audience.

Utilizing platforms strategically, such as content marketing and social media, amplifies the message and produces a symphony of brand resonance. But sales is the crescendo, while marketing is the overture. An adept sales force converts curiosity into action by utilizing tailored communication and a deep comprehension of the problems faced by customers.

Insights derived from data are the key ingredient. Analytics direct marketing plans, optimizing them for optimal effect, while sales teams use client information to craft persuasive sales presentations. Selling a product is only one aspect of communication; another is creating a narrative that a buyer wants to be a part of.

Agility plays a vital role in this healthy relationship. Achieving a performance that is meaningful in the dynamic business environment requires embracing innovative technology, responding to changes in the market, and fine-tuning tactics based on immediate feedback. When combined, strong sales and marketing generate more than simply financial gains; they also leave a lasting impression on consumers, turning them into devoted followers and brand ambassadors.

# Six Causes Your Company Isn't Making Sales and How to Address Them

There Are Currently or Soon Too Many Issues with Your Company.

It may seem that the best moment to sell a company is when you're having trouble making ends meet or when you anticipate an event that will negatively affect your revenue. That being said, you never want to sell a company "at the bottom," just like you would with stocks.

The Owner Experience Needed for the Business Is Too Great

Could someone with leadership experience replace you if you were to leave tomorrow? How can someone purchase and run your firm if it is dependent on you for operations?

## *Your Company Is Not Prepared for the Marketplace*

You're not necessarily ready to hand over the controls just because there aren't any red lights in the cockpit. Even if your company is extremely successful, it will struggle in the marketplace.

### *The Company Cannot Grow*

Your company's revenue does not guarantee future growth, even if it is great now. Not only should desirable firms provide consistent revenue, but they should also cultivate a clear route to increase revenue.

### *The company only serves one or two sizable clients, or they are all your friends.*

When 60 percent or more of a business depends on a single customer, buyers become uneasy. You most likely won't have a business left if you lose that client. If the majority of your customers are your close pals, it's practically worse.

### *Your Company Is Not Well Promoted*

It can be challenging to sell Internet firms, particularly those in the lower mid-market. Working with a traditional brokerage is probably not what you want to do because they typically charge up to 12 percent of the transaction price for businesses that sell for less than $1 million. You can't always be sure how many customers you'll reach, and the fees can mount up even if you're selling just above this valuation.

### *Your Price Request Is Too High*

Being the founder of your company makes it difficult to evaluate its value objectively. It's possible that you invested years in growing it from a failing product to a successful enterprise. Perhaps the only reason you're selling is financial hardship—a tree falling on your property, for example—or the necessity to receive medical attention.

# Chapter Six

## Overview of the process of closure

In a business setting, the closing procedure signifies the end of a deal or transaction and the last stages lead to the transfer of ownership or the signing of a contract. Legal requirements and careful attention to detail are required during this crucial stage. Fundamentally, the closing procedure seeks to guarantee that both parties complete their end of the bargain and that all prerequisites have been satisfied.

Finalizing legal documents, such as contracts and transfer agreements, and conducting a thorough examination to ensure accuracy are essential elements. During this stage, financial settlements are carried out, such as asset allocation, payment of existing debts, and fund transfers. Professionals from the legal, financial, and occasionally regulatory sectors are present during the closing.

During the closing process, parties must communicate to address any potential concerns and to clarify any last-minute questions. There may be a transitional phase following closing during which the new owners take over management and operational duties. A smooth and well-coordinated process is crucial since a successful closure signifies the start of a new chapter for all parties involved, not just a contractual formality.

## Getting the closure ready

Whether it's for a real estate deal, business sale, or contract, getting ready for closing is a detailed procedure that includes a few essential stages to guarantee a seamless and successful transition. ***Here's a thorough how-to for getting ready for the closing:***

- **Review of Documentation:**

Examine any pertinent papers in detail, such as financial accounts, contracts, and agreements. Verify the fulfillment of all prerequisites for the closing and settle any unresolved matters.

- **Adherence to the Law:**

Verify that all rules and regulations are being followed. As you ensure that the transaction complies with local laws and industry standards, take care of any legal issues or unresolved matters.

- **Money Settlements:**

Arrange money, confirm payment options, and make sure everyone understands their financial obligations to be ready for financial settlements. Pay your taxes, debts, and any due financial commitments.

- **Creating the Closing Statement:**

Make a thorough closing statement that summarizes the transaction's financial information. A summary of expenses, any necessary modifications, and the total amount to be traded should all be included in this document.

- **Working Together with Experts:** Collaborate closely with financial advisors, attorneys, and any other pertinent specialists. Make sure that everyone is on the same page on the closing procedure and ready to handle any possible unforeseen problems.

- **Planning Communications:** Create a communication strategy to inform all parties involved at every stage of the closure. This includes informing the staff, clients, and any other pertinent parties of the impending changes.

- **Last-minute Property Exams:** Make sure the property satisfies the agreed-upon conditions by conducting final property inspections for real estate transactions. Take care of any last-minute issues or required maintenance.

- **Getting the Required Approvals:**

Obtain the necessary consents or approvals from shareholders, regulatory agencies, and other pertinent parties. Make sure the required documents have all the required signatures on them.

- **Final Inspections:**

Verify that every detail of the transaction complies with the terms that were agreed upon by doing final walkthroughs or inspections. This is especially crucial to verify the property's condition in real estate transactions.

- **Logistics of Closing Day:**

Arrange the closing day's details, such as the venue, the time, and any special needs. Verify that the closing documents are ready for execution and that all relevant parties are present or represented.

- **After-Closing Monitoring:**

Create a follow-up plan for after the closing to handle any unresolved issues that might come up after the transaction is finished. This could entail attending to staff grievances, completing any outstanding documentation, or handling any unforeseen problems.

***The key to a successful closing is meticulous planning.***

# How a Sales is Closed

Even little advice can have a major impact on closing transactions. View the most beneficial closing advice below.

**#1: Determine the needs of the client.**

First things first, make sure you specify exactly what needs your product or service is meant to fulfill for the customer. Clients that are not a good fit for your offerings are not interested in hearing from you. It will be a waste of your time and money to pursue them.

Once the needs or pain areas of your customers are well-defined, you can identify specific prospects and companies that meet those needs. It will be interesting for these prospective clients to hear from you.

**#2: Locate the decision-maker.**

Long before a customer signs a contract, the sale must be closed. Qualification of leads is the initial task.

Speak with decision-makers who are crucial to the purchase of your good or service by qualifying leads. You need to create an ideal customer profile (ICP) to accomplish this.

*When creating your ICP, incorporate details such as:*

**Sector:** Determine which sectors your product will work best in.

**Company size:** Indicate the ideal staffing level for a certain organization.

**Location:** Indicate where your audience is located.

**Income:** Establish a revenue threshold at which a business is suitable for your solution.

**Job title:** Enumerate the typical job titles that your ideal client holds.

## #3: Start a discussion.

Use resources like Hunter and Snov to locate and confirm the email addresses of your leads once you've located them. By doing this, you can send emails to leads that won't end up in their spam folder.

Write, edit, and send a succinct cold email with a call-to-action that doesn't promote your product after the email address has been verified. Getting the prospective customer to set up a conversation or to reply favorably to your email should be your main objective.

## #4: Outline the advantages of your offering.

Reaching out to potential customers via phone or email is just half the fight. The impact of your product on your prospect's business operations is demonstrated in the second half.

Avoid the error of pitching prospects based solely on features. Let them see the advantages of utilizing your offering. When you do, people will witness the problems your product resolves and the observable effects of using it.

## #5:  Make things feel urgent.

To keep your agreements from stagnating or collapsing, you must create a feeling of urgency. Prospects have an incentive to proceed with a deal when there is urgency.

Offering a limited-time discount, free onboarding, or anything else that enables the prospect to benefit from your solution right away will help you generate urgency.

## #6: Be ready to handle any objections that may arise

Having objections can be beneficial. An objection indicates that your potential customer wants to proceed but is having concerns. By addressing these criticisms, you will move closer to meeting your quota.

***Typical objections a salesperson may encounter are as follows:***

There isn't time.

We lack the necessary funds.

Your merchandise is pricey.

We don't currently require your goods.

I have to talk to my significant other or another decision-maker.

# Chapter Seven

## Resilience and Collaboration

"Give Back and Network Up" is a twofold attitude that goes beyond just professional tactics; it's a potent tenet for long-term success and significant effect. A key component of community enrichment is giving back, whether it takes the form of mentoring, blog contributions, or knowledge-sharing in forums. By giving freely of your knowledge, you improve your field and establish yourself as a reliable and cooperative leader.

Concurrently, networking entails creating relationships with significant figures in your industry. These connections act as a springboard for priceless mentoring, calculated alliances, and joint ventures that elevate your career. Interacting with powerful people not only opens doors but also offers chances to have a larger impact.

Giving back and networking together produce a harmonious synergy that increases the reach and effect of your community initiatives. It's a positive feedback loop where your kindness makes others around you better, and your smart networking puts you in front of influential people in the field, creating a vibrant environment that encourages development and cooperation. By adopting this philosophy, you promote a culture of group empowerment and achievement in addition to helping others climb the success ladder.

Being a mentor and giving back to the community.

Being a mentor is a transforming act that gives back to the community by fostering a legacy of growth and empowerment in addition to imparting information. Mentorship is more than just a transactional relationship; it is a commitment to the personal growth of community members. Mentors become the architects of their mentees' professional and personal success by providing direction, wisdom, and encouragement.

Mentoring is a two-way street; as mentors impart their knowledge and experience, they also pick up new insights that enliven their comprehension of their subject. A collaborative atmosphere is fostered by this reciprocal interchange, which builds a strong community of learners.

Trust is the money and wisdom is the gift in the mentoring journey. Mentors shape the next generation of leaders and innovators, benefiting not only the present but also the future. It's a cascading effect, where mentoring has an impact on the community .

# Establishing relationships with key people in your industry

Establishing connections with prominentas a whole, not just on specific individuals. Within the mentoring community, providing becomes a legacy, a reflection of the idea that communities thrive best when information is freely exchanged and group development is given top priority.

 figures within your industry is a crucial element for career advancement, providing access to prospects that might otherwise stay unattainable. Establishing intentional and purposeful connections with business leaders is an art that goes beyond simple socializing and has the power to influence your professional path.

First of all, powerful people frequently have a plethora of knowledge and wisdom. Making relationships with them gives you access to a wealth of information that can provide direction, coaching, and original viewpoints. These connections act as a compass, assisting you in navigating the nuances of your industry and offering a successful path forward.

Additionally, networking with powerful people has a cascading impact. As you integrate into their professional network, your industry visibility and trustworthiness increase. Increased visibility can result in speaking engagements, project collaborations, and invitations to special events, all of which can help you progress professionally.

Forming strategic partnerships with powerful people also promotes a feeling of support and community. Being a part of a network where communication is open and teamwork thrives fosters an environment where success is shared by everybody. Not only is it vital to know what you know, but also, and perhaps more significantly, who you know.

In the era of digital technology, networking now takes place in virtual places in addition to actual gatherings. Interacting with prominent figures in the industry via social media, professional networks, and online discussion boards facilitates a worldwide network that cuts over geographic borders.

To initiate fruitful networking with powerful people, approach conversations with sincerity and a sincere desire to learn. Join pertinent professional groups, take part in webinars, and attend industry conferences. Building relationships can begin with a casual chat and develop into a partnership, mentoring, or even friendship that benefits your personal and professional lives.

Essentially, cultivating a network of prominent people is a calculated investment in your career path. It's about creating connections that go beyond transactional exchanges and support a vibrant, cooperative professional ecosystem where possibilities abound and success is shared.

# Concluding Remarks

Become the Wealthy Catalyst plays a transformational tune that goes beyond monetary achievement in the symphony of success. It's about leading a symphony of strategic thinking, entrepreneurial energy, and purpose-driven success rather than just amassing cash.

As we come to the end of this guide, try to picture yourself as a dynamic force that is reshaping communities and industries rather than just a financial heavyweight. The Wealthy Catalyst has an entrepreneurial attitude that transforms obstacles into opportunities as they deftly negotiate the complex dance of job options.

Financial mastery combines strategic financial intelligence, astute investing, and wealth generation into an art form. However, the Rich Catalyst doesn't hoard success; instead, they leave a lasting legacy that goes beyond balance sheets by giving liberally to their industry and community.

Shaking hands with powerful people is only one aspect of networking; another is a smart dance that opens doors to opportunities and collaborations that advance your career. Staying on the cutting edge of knowledge and innovation is ensured by continuous learning, which becomes a lifelong friend.

Recall that this grand finale is a purpose-driven story about being the Wealthy Catalyst. It's about giving your work purpose and making a lasting impression on the future generation and your industry. It's a customized path that combines material wealth with power and impact, causing success to spread.

Therefore, picture your legacy as a collaborative symphony where positive change is catalyzed by your accomplishment rather than as a solo triumph. Become the Rich Catalyst, not only for the money you accumulate but also for the lasting legacy and revolutionary power you will possess. Your story doesn't end here; it reverberates across your town, through the halls of industry, and into the hearts of those who are moved by your bold pursuit of prosperity and meaning.